For Jessica, Julia, & Nikki, who always believed
that their dad was worth listening to.
-Tim Jantzi, M.Ed.

For Dorothy, who inspires me and supported
my dreams even when we were eating tuna mac
three nights a week.
-Alex Smith

OUT-THINKING
The 7 Lies
About
SCHOOL

Written by:

Tim Jantzi, M. Ed.

Illustrated by:

Alex Smith

RULER OF THE UNIVERSE!

JANTZI
Test Prep, Inc.
STRATEGIES FOR SUCCESS

PROUDLY PRESENTS:

OUT-THINKING
The 7 Lies
About
SCHOOL

WORDS - TIM JANTZI, M.ED.
PICTURES - ALEX SMITH

(3.)

I'VE ALWAYS BEEN AMAZED AT THE 3" THICK SAT PREP BOOKS SOLD IN STORES BECAUSE I KNOW KIDS DON'T EVEN LOOK AT THEM. I KNOW YOUR MOM BOUGHT IT HOPING YOU'D CRACK IT OPEN.

WRONG KIND OF CRACK, MOM.

WELCOME TO YOUR REALITY.

I'M GOING TO GET TO THE POINT *RIGHT NOW*. I KNOW THIS BOOK WILL HELP YOU, BUT I'VE GOT TO MAKE IT READABLE (FUNNY) TO KEEP YOUR ATTENTION. I'LL DO THAT.

HERE'S WHAT I PROMISE: IF YOU READ AND DO THESE THINGS I TELL YOU, YOU CAN START DOING WHAT YOU WANT TO DO. YOU CAN GET YOUR PARENTS *OFF YOUR BACK*. THE PAIN CAN STOP. AFTER ALL, THAT'S REALLY WHAT THIS IS ALL ABOUT.

YEAH, YOU CARE ABOUT YOUR GRADES AND SCHOOL, BUT NOT AS MUCH YOU CARE ABOUT YOUR NEXT TEXT, EMAIL OR WHATEVER. SO HOW CAN I HELP YOU?

THAT'S EASY: *I KNOW EVERYTHING.*

JANTZI $M\bar{c}^2$

NO, I'M SERIOUS.

SO HERE'S THE DEAL...

...I'M GOING TO TELL YOU EVERYTHING YOU NEED TO BE MASSIVELY, RIDULOUSLY SUCCESSFUL IN SCHOOL SO YOU CAN GET BACK TO WHAT *YOU* WANT TO DO.

BECAUSE IT'S ALL ABOUT *YOU*, REMEMBER? ADMIT IT.

RIGHT NOW YOU'RE SAYING:

WHY DOES HE THINK HE KNOWS WHAT I'M THINKING?

BECAUSE I'VE TAUGHT A GAZILLION KIDS LIKE YOU!

BUT I'M DIFFERENT!

ARE YOU NOW?

OF COURSE I AM.

NO, YOU'RE NOT, AND I'LL PROVE IT TO YOU.

HAVE YOU EVER BEEN ASSIGNED A PAPER, PROJECT, ETC. TO DO A MONTH IN ADVANCE, AND THEN WRITTEN THE WHOLE THING THE NIGHT BEFORE? HOW MANY TIMES HAVE YOU SPENT THE WHOLE NIGHT STUDYING FOR A TEST AND STILL GOT A LOUSY GRADE? C'MON, YOU'VE GOT THE ATTENTION SPAN OF A GNAT

YOU'RE NOT DIFFERENT. RIGHT NOW YOU'RE IN A PREDICAMENT. YOU'VE GOT TWO CHOICES: STICK WITH YOUR STUPID PRIDE AND FLOUNDER, OR *STAY WITH ME* AND HAVE A CHANCE AT IMPROVEMENT. YOU CAN GET BACK TO WHAT YOU WERE DOING, OR YOU CAN MAKE THINGS A LOT BETTER.

NOW THAT THE ONE-WAY LOVE FEST IS OVER, I WANT YOU TO TRUST ME. WHY? BECAUSE YOU DON'T HAVE ANY REAL CHOICE. IF YOU DON'T, YOU'RE SCREWED. IF YOU DON'T, I CAN'T HELP YOU.

YOU'RE NOT HAPPY RIGHT NOW, AND IT'S MOSTLY BECAUSE SCHOOL ISN'T GOING THE WAY YOU WANT. YOU MIGHT BE TRYING HARD, BUT YOU AND I KNOW YOU'RE JUST SPINNING YOUR WHEELS. YOU'RE NOT REALLY GETTING ANYWHERE, ARE YOU?

UH, NOT REALLY.

YOU KNOW WHAT I MEAN BY GETTING AHEAD; YOU WOULDN'T MIND GETTING BETTER GRADES, BUT YOU REALLY FEEL LIKE IT SHOULD BE EASIER.

NOW, SOME OF YOU READING THIS BOOK ARE HARD-CORE AND SCHOOL IS GOING PRETTY WELL, THANK YOU VERY MUCH. *KEEP READING.* YOU MAY THINK BY THE WAY I'M TALKING THAT I THINK ALL STUDENTS ARE SLACK. THEY'RE NOT...

JUST *MOST* OF THEM.

YOU MAY ALSO THINK THAT YOU ALREADY KNOW WHAT I'M GOING TO TALK ABOUT, BUT YOU DON'T. NO CHANCE! SO, NOW THAT I'VE GOT EVERYONE ON BOARD, LET'S DO THIS. READY?

JANTZI LOVES YOU.

BTW, IT'S PROBABLY TIME YOU BOUGHT THIS BOOK. IF YOU'VE READ THIS FAR, I'M MAKING SENSE, WHICH MEANS I CAN HELP YOU.

BESIDES, THAT LADY OVER THERE WITH THE NAME-TAG IS IN DANGER OF PERMANENT FACIAL DISFIGURATION FROM THE DEATH STARE SHE'S GIVING YOU.

I'M SORRY, I'M JUST A LITTLE SURPRISED.
NOT KNOWING THE QUESTION IS LIKE
SOMEONE WALKING INTO ROOM WITH A KNIFE
IN HIS BACK, RESPONDING TO EVERYONE'S
HORROR WITH, "WHAT KNIFE?"

SO...*WHY DO YOU HAVE TO LEARN THIS STUFF?* HERE'S THE 3 PART ANSWER:

1. SO YOUR BRAIN WON'T SHRIVEL UP AND DIE FOR THE NEXT FEW YEARS (LIFE SUPPORT).

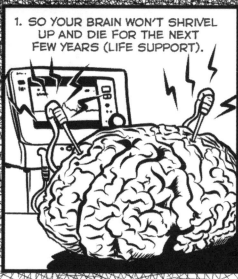

2. BECAUSE WE'RE EXPOSING YOU TO EVERYTHING TO SEE WHAT STICKS (STUFF HITTING THE FAN).

3. ADULTS THINK IT'S FUN TO SEE YOU STRUGGLE... JUST KIDDING! ...SORT OF. THE LAST REASON WE STUFF ALL OF THIS INTO YOUR PUNY BRAIN IS THAT WE'RE TRYING HELP YOU LEARN *HOW TO LEARN.*

(13.)

HAVE YOU EVER HEARD ABOUT STUFF *HITTING THE FAN?*

WHY ARE THEY THROWING STUFF AT A FAN ANYWAYS?

IN HIGH SCHOOL, THEY THROW ALL THIS *CRAP* AT YOU AND SOMETHING IS BOUND TO STICK TO THE FAN. THEN YOU MIGHT TURN WHATEVER STICKS INTO A CAREER.

THINK ABOUT CHOOSING A MAJOR FOR COLLEGE. YOU START BY THINKING ABOUT SUBJECTS IN SCHOOL AND YOU SAY, "MAN, I *HATED* THAT CLASS" OR "THAT ONE *SUCKED.*" UNTIL YOU SETTLE ON THE ONE YOU HATED THE *LEAST* (NOT COUNTING LUNCH).

I CHOSE TO STUDY BIOLOGY IN COLLEGE BECAUSE I KNEW FROM MY EXPERIENCES IN HIGH SCHOOL THAT IT WOULD SUCK *A LOT* LESS THAN MY OTHER CHOICES.

IT'S A REAL *GIFT FROM GOD* IF YOU ARE *ABSOLUTELY* SURE OF WHAT YOU WANT TO DO WITH THE REST OF YOUR LIFE BY THE TENTH GRADE. THIS WILL *PROBABLY* CHANGE ANYWAY, BUT AT LEAST YOU HAVE DIRECTION - *OR THE ILLUSION OF IT.*

YOUR TEACHERS EXPOSE YOU TO ALL OF THIS BORING STUFF IN HIGH SCHOOL IN THE HOPES THAT AT LEAST *ONE ASPECT* OF IT WILL BE REMOTELY INTERESTING ENOUGH THAT YOU COULD TURN IT INTO A JOB YOU'LL *ACTUALLY ENJOY* SOMEDAY. IF ALL ELSE FAILS, YOU CAN ALWAYS BE A LIBERAL ARTS MAJOR AND HOOK YOURSELF UP TO *ACADEMIC LIFE SUPPORT* FOR ANOTHER FOUR YEARS.

THE 7 LIES THAT ARE RUINING YOUR ACADEMIC CAREER

HERE ARE THE SEVEN MOST POPULAR LIES THAT KEEP STUDENTS FROM SUCCEEDING:

1. YOU'LL MISS OUT ON EVERYTHING

2. NOBODY LIKES THE SMART KID

3. YOU'LL TURN INTO YOUR PARENTS' LAP-DOG

4. YOU'RE ALREADY SMART ENOUGH

5. YOU'RE NOT SMART ENOUGH

6. YOU'RE GONNA BE A SUPER-STAR

7. PEER PRESSURE IS BAD

IF YOU BELIEVE *ANY* OF THESE LIES, THEN YOU'VE GOT IT ALL *SDRAWKCAB!!* SOMEBODY NEEDS TO SMACK YOU UPSIDE THE HEAD.

DON'T WORRY - THAT'S WHAT I'M HERE FOR!

LIE 1: YOU'LL MISS OUT ON EVERYTHING

MANY STUDENTS BELIEVE THAT IF YOU DO YOUR SCHOOL WORK FIRST YOU'LL BE CHEATING YOURSELF OUT OF DOING STUFF WITH YOUR FRIENDS. THAT'S SO STUPID, DUDE! I MEAN WHO *ARE* YOU? ARE YOU SUCH A MINDLESS ZOMBIE THAT YOU WOULD *EVER* FORGET TO HANG WITH YOUR FRIENDS?

NO WAY. YOU WILL *ALWAYS* MAKE TIME FOR THAT. WHAT I'M TALKING ABOUT IS A LITTLE SHIFT IN TIMING.

LOOK, SCHOOL IS AN INESCAPABLE REALITY. YOU GOTTA GO TO SCHOOL & THERE'S GOING TO BE SOME WORK.

I'M JUST SUGGESTING YOU ADJUST *WHEN* YOU DO IT. BESIDES, WHEN WAS THE LAST TIME YOU MISSED OUT ON SOMETHING BIG *BECAUSE OF SCHOOL?*

I DON'T REMEMBER

SO THE *TRUTH IS* THAT THE WHOLE "MISSING OUT ON STUFF" THING NEVER HAPPENS. 'CUZ YOU WON'T LET IT.

NOW, EVERY ONCE IN A WHILE SOMETHING LAST MINUTE WILL COME UP, AND IT'S A TIGHT SQUEEZE TO DO BOTH, BUT THAT'S 'CUZ YOU PROCRASTINATE.

NAME THREE THINGS YOU WANT TO DO WITH YOUR FRIENDS THIS WEEK.

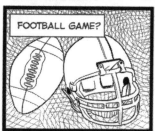

FOOTBALL GAME?

BIG PARTY?

NEWEST MOVIE?

REGARDLESS OF HOW MUCH SCHOOLWORK YOU HAVE, YOU'RE *GOING* TO DO THESE THINGS.

WOULD YOU ENJOY THEM MORE IF YOUR SCHOOLWORK WAS *DONE?* OR WOULD YOU *RATHER* GO TO THESE EVENTS WITH *SCHOOL* IN THE BACK OF YOUR MIND?

THINK ABOUT IT THIS WAY: IF AN EMPLOYEE SHOWED UP AT WORK ON MONDAY MORNING AND EXPECTED HIS CHECK *FIRST*, BEFORE HE PUT IN HIS 40 HOURS, YOU'D THINK HE WAS *CRAZY.* YET, THAT IS WHAT MOST STUDENTS DO. THEY GO OUT WITH THEIR FRIENDS, DO *WHATEVER THEY WANT*, AND PUT OFF THEIR SCHOOL WORK UNTIL THE END. THAT'S WHY STUDENTS *RESENT* SCHOOLWORK; THEY'VE ALREADY CASHED THEIR CHECK, & NOW THEY OWE THE MAN.

WHAT WOULD HAPPEN IF TONIGHT FOR DINNER YOU SAT DOWN AND ATE THREE BOWLS OF ICE CREAM AND THEN YOUR MOM MADE YOU EAT A PLATE OF BROCCOLI?

THAT WOULD SUCK!

NOW FLIP IT AROUND. THIS TIME YOUR MOM BRINGS YOU THE BROCCOLI FIRST. YOU COULD THROW SOME RANCH ON IT OR SMOTHER IT IN CHEESE & GET IT OUT OF THE WAY. AT LEAST YOU'VE GOT ICE CREAM TO LOOK FORWARD TO AFTER-WARDS. THAT'S WHY THEY CALL IT DESSERT!

ITS THE SAME WAY WITH SCHOOLWORK. YOU HAVE TO DO IT AT SOME POINT...

...BUT GETTING IT OUT OF THE WAY MAKES LIFE *SO MUCH* EASIER.

NOW WE CAN MOVE ON TO MOTIVATION.

WELL, I'M ALL RIGHT THERE.

I'M SORRY, YOUR MOTIVATION IS *FINE?!?* THEN WHY DO YOU SPEND 3/4 OF YOUR TIME THINKING ABOUT SCHOOL STUFF AND 1/4 DOING IT?

DO YOU THINK I'M AN *IDIOT?* DON'T ANSWER THAT! *YOUR MOTIVATION SUCKS.*

LIE 2:
NOBODY LIKES THE SMART KID.

SO THE SMARTEST KID IN YOUR SCHOOL HAS NO FRIENDS, AND YOU'RE WORRIED THAT IF YOU GET TOO SMART, YOU WON'T HAVE ANY EITHER. WELL, TRUST ME, YOU WON'T BE EATING YOUR LUNCH ALONE IN A BATHROOM STALL IF YOU START GETTING A'S; NOT IF YOU DO IT THE RIGHT WAY.

THE TRUTH IS THAT SOME OF THE KIDS WHO GET RIDICULOUSLY GOOD GRADES DON'T HAVE MANY FRIENDS BECAUSE FRIEND-SHIP TAKES TIME.

MANY OF THEM HAVEN'T FIGURED OUT HOW TO BALANCE THEIR PRIORITIES; THEY'RE SPENDING ALL OF THEIR TIME ON SCHOOLWORK & POINTLESS RESUME-BUILDING EXTRA-CURRICULARS.

BTW - COLLEGES DON'T REALLY CARE ABOUT THEM (SEE MORE ON TIME-MANAGEMENT IN BOOK 2).

OTHER BRAINIACS DON'T HAVE FRIENDS BECAUSE THEY FEEL IT'S NECCESSARY TO CUT THROATS TO GET AHEAD.

THEY ARE LOST SOULS.

EVERYONE SHOULD KNOW THAT ONLY SALUTATORIANS ARE JUSTIFIED IN DOING SUCH THINGS.

AFTER ALL, SECOND PLACE IS JUST THE FIRST TO LOSE!

STILL OTHER SMART KIDS JUST PLAIN DON'T KNOW HOW TO MAKE FRIENDS. EVEN IF YOU GOT BETTER AT SCHOOL THAT WOULDN'T HAPPEN TO YOU, BECAUSE YOU'RE YOU. YOU'RE NOT LIKELY TO LOSE YOURSELF IN SCHOOLWORK, YOU WON'T CUT THROATS, AND YOU KNOW HOW TO MAKE & KEEP FRIENDS.

HOWEVER, SOME OF THE SMART KIDS DO HAVE FRIENDS: THE OTHER *SO-CALLED* NERDS.

I'M NOT INTERESTED IN JOINING THE ROLLING BOOKBAG CLUB

HANG ON A SECOND. *I WAS A NERD* IN COLLEGE.

YOU WERE?

YEAH, BY "BEING A NERD" I MEAN I *LEARNED A LOT* IN COLLEGE, TREATED IT LIKE *A JOB*, & THEREFORE EXERCISED *TOTAL DOMINION* OVER MY KINGDOM. BY THE WAY, THOSE KIDS WITH THE ROLLING BOOKBAGS WILL BE LAUGHING WHEN YOU'RE *CRIPPLED* WITH SCOLIOSIS AT AGE 40.

HERE'S THE *LIE* THAT YOU BELIEVE: *NERDS = LOSERS.* WRONG! NERDS *RULE THE WORLD.* N.E.R.D. IS AN ACRONYM THAT STANDS FOR:

NEVER

ENDING

RULE &

DOMINION

WHEN SMART KIDS ARE 15 THEY MIGHT BE CALLED NERDS, BUT WHEN THEY'RE 30 THEY GET CALLED *DIFFERENT* NAMES, LIKE: *BOSS, CEO, MR. PRESIDENT.* THEY ARE SO SUCCESSFUL, THEY GET FRIENDS THE OLD FASHIONED WAY: THEY *BUY* THEM!

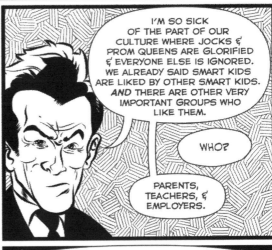

I'M SO SICK OF THE PART OF OUR CULTURE WHERE JOCKS & PROM QUEENS ARE GLORIFIED & EVERYONE ELSE IS IGNORED. WE ALREADY SAID SMART KIDS ARE LIKED BY OTHER SMART KIDS. *AND* THERE ARE OTHER VERY IMPORTANT GROUPS WHO LIKE THEM.

WHO?

PARENTS, TEACHERS, & EMPLOYERS.

PEOPLE WHO HAVE THE POWER AND RESOURCES TO HOOK YOU UP! I *LOVE* THE WORD "RESOURCES," BECAUSE IT MEANS A SOURCE YOU CAN *KEEP* USING.

LIKE A WELL WITHOUT A BOTTOM.

BUT *BY FAR*, THE PERSON WHO LIKES IT WHEN KIDS *BUST THEIR BUTTS* IN SCHOOL IS...

...JANTZI!

LET ME CLUE YOU IN HERE - IF YOUR FRIENDS CHOOSE NOT TO HANG OUT WITH YOU ANYMORE BECAUSE YOU START DOING BETTER IN SCHOOL, JUST WAIT...

...PEOPLE HANG OUT WITH PEOPLE WHO ARE LIKE THEM, WHO DO THE SAME THINGS THEY DO & BELIEVE THE THINGS THEY BELIEVE. SO IF YOU START TRYING HARDER IN SCHOOL AND MAKING YOUR ACADEMIC GOALS HIGHER ON YOUR PRIORITY LIST, YOUR GROUP OF FRIENDS MIGHT CHANGE... BECAUSE *YOU* MIGHT CHANGE.

CHANGE IS INEVITABLE AND CAN BE GOOD IF YOU'RE DOING THE CHOOSING. YOU MUST BE OPEN TO THAT OR YOU WOULDN'T BE READING THIS. YOUR REAL FRIENDS WILL STILL BE THERE IF THEY'RE FRIENDS WORTH HAVING!

TIME FOR...
ANOTHER
TRUE STORY OF
JANTZI

WHEN I WAS 4 YEARS OLD MY BROTHERS PUT ME IN THE DRYER. THEY WERE TRYING TO GET BACK AT THE BABYSITTER FOR TELLING US WE COULDN'T HAVE ICE CREAM. WHAT BETTER WAY TO GET THE BABYSITTER IN TROUBLE THAN BY KILLING YOUR BROTHER? INCIDENTS LIKE THIS WERE, SADLY, A COMMON OCCURRENCE IN MY CHILDHOOD. IT BEGAN WITH MY BROTHERS TELLING ME THAT THEY HAD ICE CREAM DOWNSTAIRS, AND I, NATURALLY, BELIEVED THEM. WHEN WE GOT DOWN THERE THEY SAID THEY COULD HEAR THE BABYSITTER COMING SO WE ALL HAD TO HIDE. THEY ENTHUSIASTICALLY SUGGESTED THAT I JUMP IN THE DRYER, AND THEY "HELPED" ME GET IN. AFTER SHUTTING THE DRYER DOOR THEY QUICKLY MOVED SOMETHING HEAVY IN FRONT OF IT SO THAT I COULDN'T GET OUT. THEN THEY TURNED IT ON. THEY YELLED TO ME THAT I'D BE FINE —IT WAS ONLY SET TO PERMANENT PRESS.

LIE

LIE 3:
YOU'LL TURN INTO YOUR PARENTS' LAPDOG

I'LL TELL YOU A STORY THAT SHOULD HELP YOU IF YOUR PARENTS ARE RIDING YOU. ONE DAY IN GYM CLASS WE HAD TO DO TWENTY-FIVE PUSH-UPS.

WHAT DOES THIS HAVE TO DO WITH NAGGING?

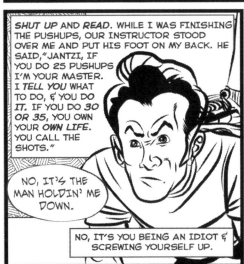

SHUT UP AND *READ*. WHILE I WAS FINISHING THE PUSHUPS, OUR INSTRUCTOR STOOD OVER ME AND PUT HIS FOOT ON MY BACK. HE SAID, "JANTZI, IF YOU DO 25 PUSHUPS I'M YOUR MASTER. I *TELL YOU* WHAT TO DO, & YOU DO *IT*. IF YOU DO *30 OR 35*, YOU OWN YOUR *OWN LIFE*. YOU CALL THE SHOTS."

NO, IT'S THE MAN HOLDIN' ME DOWN.

NO, IT'S YOU BEING AN IDIOT & SCREWING YOURSELF UP.

ONE P.O.W. IN VIETNAM DID THE SAME THING IN REVERSE. HE WAS PUT IN A 5'X5' CELL AND COULD NEVER TAKE MORE THAN THREE STEPS IN ANY DIRECTION. SO, THIS GUY CHOSE TO TAKE TWO. *ONLY TWO*. THEN HE WAS MAKING THE DECISION TO LIMIT *HIMSELF*, NOT HIS CAPTORS.

HOW DOES THAT APPLY TO SCHOOL?

IT APPLIES TO EVERYTHING! YOU CAN WAIT TO TAKE ORDERS FROM OTHERS, OR YOU CAN GET AFTER IT ON YOUR OWN.

DID IT EVER OCCUR TO YOU THAT WHEN YOUR PARENTS NAG YOU, IT'S *YOUR* FAULT?

MY FAULT?!?

THINK ABOUT SOMETHING YOUR PARENTS ARE ALWAYS REPEATING AD NAUSEUM WHEN THEY NAG YOU. *"ROBBY! CLEAN YOUR ROOM!!"* WAS I CLOSE? YOU KNOW WHAT THEY'RE GOING TO SAY *EVERY* TIME. WHY? BECAUSE THEY'VE SAID THEM 26,000 TIMES!

I'M NOT GONNA LET THEM *BOSS* ME AROUND!

HOW'S THAT WORKING OUT FOR YOU?

I STILL WANNA SHOOT MYSELF IN THE FACE.

DO YOU KNOW WHAT A *PRE-EMPTIVE STRIKE* IS?

IT'S WHEN YOU TAKE *AGRESSIVE ACTION* IN SELF-DEFENSE BECAUSE YOU KNOW YOUR ENEMIES ARE FIXIN' TO *HIT YOU HARD.*

ANGER ISSUES AGAIN, JANTZI.

NOPE, COMMON SELF-PRESERVATION.

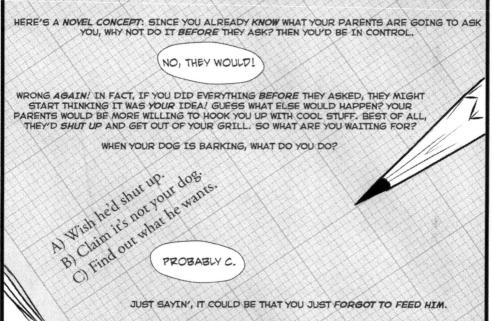

HERE'S A *NOVEL CONCEPT*: SINCE YOU ALREADY *KNOW* WHAT YOUR PARENTS ARE GOING TO ASK YOU, WHY NOT DO IT *BEFORE* THEY ASK? THEN YOU'D BE IN CONTROL.

NO, THEY WOULD!

WRONG *AGAIN!* IN FACT, IF YOU DID EVERYTHING *BEFORE* THEY ASKED, THEY MIGHT START THINKING IT WAS *YOUR* IDEA! GUESS WHAT ELSE WOULD HAPPEN? YOUR PARENTS WOULD BE MORE WILLING TO HOOK YOU UP WITH COOL STUFF. BEST OF ALL, THEY'D *SHUT UP* AND GET OUT OF YOUR GRILL. SO WHAT ARE YOU WAITING FOR?

WHEN YOUR DOG IS BARKING, WHAT DO YOU DO?

A) Wish he'd shut up.
B) Claim it's not your dog.
C) Find out what he wants.

PROBABLY C.

JUST SAYIN', IT COULD BE THAT YOU JUST *FORGOT TO FEED HIM.*

THAT WAS PRETTY *STUPID* WASN'T IT? HE GETS HUNGRY EVERY DAY DOESN'T HE? WELL, IF YOU'D FED HIM THIS MORNING, YOU WOULDN'T HAVE HAD TO DEAL WITH HIS BARKING IN THE FIRST PLACE. YOU SEE WHERE I'M GOING WITH THIS, RIGHT?

YOU WANT ME TO FEED MY *DOG?*

I WANT YOU TO THROW YOUR PARENTS A BONE ALREADY.

LIE

LIE 4:
YOU'RE ALREADY SMART ENOUGH.

WHAT IF YOUR GRADES WERE GOOD ENOUGH TO GET YOU INTO A GOOD COLLEGE AND LAND YOU A REALLY GOOD JOB? MAYBE MONEY ISN'T A BIG MOTIVATOR FOR YOU, BUT HAVE YOU EVER CONSIDERED WHAT YOU COULD DO IF YOU HAD A LITTLE EXTRA TO SPARE? I'M SURE THERE ARE A COUPLE VILLAGES IN AFRICA THAT COULD USE A DECENT WATER PURIFICATION SYSTEM.

IF YOU'RE COMPARING YOURSELF TO OTHERS, YOU MIGHT FEEL LIKE A SLIGHTLY-BIGGER-THAN-MEDIUM-SIZED FISH IN A SMALL POND. THERE'S PLENTY OF FOOD, AND YOU'RE NOT ABOUT TO GET EATEN.

BUT JUST WAIT, KIDDO: THAT POND IS ABOUT TO GET REAL BIG, REAL QUICK. WHETHER YOU'RE DIVING INTO COLLEGE OR WORK, THE COMPETITION IS GOING TO GET PRETTY DARN FIERCE, PRETTY DARN FAST.

JUST SWIMMING ALONG WON'T CUT IT. YOU HAVE TO MAKE YOURSELF BETTER THAN THE PEOPLE AROUND YOU.

BUT IT'S NOT RIGHT TO ACT BETTER THAN OTHERS...

YOU'RE RIGHT, BUT IT'S NOT WRONG TO *BE* BETTER THAN OTHERS.

THERE YOU GO AGAIN JANTZI!

WHADDYA MEAN?

YOU SOUND ARROGANT.

I AM.

YOU ADMIT IT?

SURE, I THINK I'M BETTER THAN MOST PEOPLE! JUST NOT MORE IMPORTANT.

A.) IT'S TRUE, HAVE YOU LOOKED AROUND CLOSELY TO SEE WHO'S OUT THERE?

B.) IF I DON'T BELIEVE IN MYSELF, I'LL END UP WAITING FOR ORDERS FROM OTHERS.

C.) YOU'VE HEARD OF ME RIGHT? I MEAN YOU'RE READING MY BOOK; OF COURSE I'M BETTER.

- AND YOU CAN BE TOO.

I THOUGHT COMPETING WITH OTHERS WAS A BAD THING?

NOT FOR THE PEOPLE ON TOP IT ISN'T. DO YOU REALLY THINK I REGRET BECOMING SUCCESSFUL? NO FRICKIN' WAY.

BUT WHAT ABOUT THE PEOPLE WHO CAN'T COMPETE?

GREAT QUESTION.

YOU WANT THE TRUTH? THERE ARE TWO CATEGORIES OF PEOPLE WHO AREN'T COMPETITIVE. THOSE WHO CAN'T & THOSE WHO WON'T. CAN'T MEANS THEY HAVE SOME TYPE OF DISABILITY. WE SHOW COMPASSION FOR THEM THROUGH VOLUNTEERING AND CHARITIES. THEN THERE ARE THOSE THAT WON'T COMPETE. THEY DON'T EVEN TRY, DUDE! THESE ARE PEOPLE WITH NO VALID REASON FOR THEIR LACK OF AMBITION.

MAYBE THEY HAD A BAD CHILDHOOD.

EVERYBODY HAD A BAD CHILDHOOD! I WAS *RAISED BY WOLVES.* WHY DO YOU THINK I BECAME AN EVIL GENIUS?

ANYONE EVER TELL YOU THAT IF YOU DON'T DO YOUR BEST IN SCHOOL, YOU'LL WIND UP FLIPPING BURGERS?

WHILE THERE'S ALWAYS A CHANCE THAT COULD HAPPEN, MOST OF YOU ARE NOT ACTUALLY IN DANGER OF A LIFETIME IN THE FAST FOOD INDUSTRY. RELIEVED? DON'T BE.

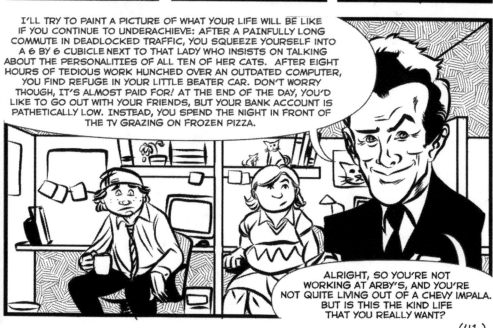

I'LL TRY TO PAINT A PICTURE OF WHAT YOUR LIFE WILL BE LIKE IF YOU CONTINUE TO UNDERACHIEVE: AFTER A PAINFULLY LONG COMMUTE IN DEADLOCKED TRAFFIC, YOU SQUEEZE YOURSELF INTO A 6 BY 6 CUBICLE NEXT TO THAT LADY WHO INSISTS ON TALKING ABOUT THE PERSONALITIES OF ALL TEN OF HER CATS. AFTER EIGHT HOURS OF TEDIOUS WORK HUNCHED OVER AN OUTDATED COMPUTER, YOU FIND REFUGE IN YOUR LITTLE BEATER CAR. DON'T WORRY THOUGH, IT'S ALMOST PAID FOR! AT THE END OF THE DAY, YOU'D LIKE TO GO OUT WITH YOUR FRIENDS, BUT YOUR BANK ACCOUNT IS PATHETICALLY LOW. INSTEAD, YOU SPEND THE NIGHT IN FRONT OF THE TV GRAZING ON FROZEN PIZZA.

ALRIGHT, SO YOU'RE NOT WORKING AT ARBY'S, AND YOU'RE NOT QUITE LIVING OUT OF A CHEVY IMPALA. BUT IS THIS THE KIND LIFE THAT YOU REALLY WANT?

(41.)

TIME FOR...

ANOTHER
TRUE STORY OF
JANTZI

I WAS PLAYING DARTS IN THE GARAGE ONE DAY WITH MY BROTHER, AND HE MANAGED TO BEAT ME. HE MADE A SORE WINNER OF HIMSELF, TALKING TRASH AND STICKING HIS TONGUE OUT AT ME SO I CHASED HIM AND CORNERED HIM IN FRONT OF A DOOR. I TRIED TO PUNCH HIM IN THE HEAD, BUT HE DUCKED AND MY FIST WENT THROUGH THE SMALL WINDOW IN THE DOOR. I PULLED MY ARM BACK THROUGH AND THERE WAS A HUGE SHARD OF GLASS LODGED IN MY WRIST. I PULLED IT OUT AND A 3 FOOT FOUNTAIN OF BLOOD STARTED GUSHING OUT ALL OVER THE PLACE. I STARTED CHASING MY BROTHER AROUND THE HOUSE SPRAYING HIM WITH BLOOD. OUR MOM CAME OUT TO SEE WHAT THE RUCKUS WAS AND THOUGHT THAT MY BROTHER WAS THE ONE BLEEDING SO SHE TOOK HIM AND PUT HIM IN THE SHOWER. AFTER 15 MINUTES OF RINSING SHE COULDN'T FIND A WOUND ON HIM, MEANWHILE I'M IN THE GARAGE SLOWLY BLEEDING TO DEATH, WITH A DIRTY SHOP RAG PRESSED INTO THE CUT. SHE CAME BACK TO TAKE ME TO THE EMERGENCY ROOM AND AS THE CAR WAS PULLING OUT MY BROTHER CAME UP AND STUCK HIS TONGUE OUT AT ME AGAIN. I ROLLED DOWN THE WINDOW AND SPRAYED ANOTHER GUSH OF BLOOD INTO HIS FRESHLY CLEANED FACE.

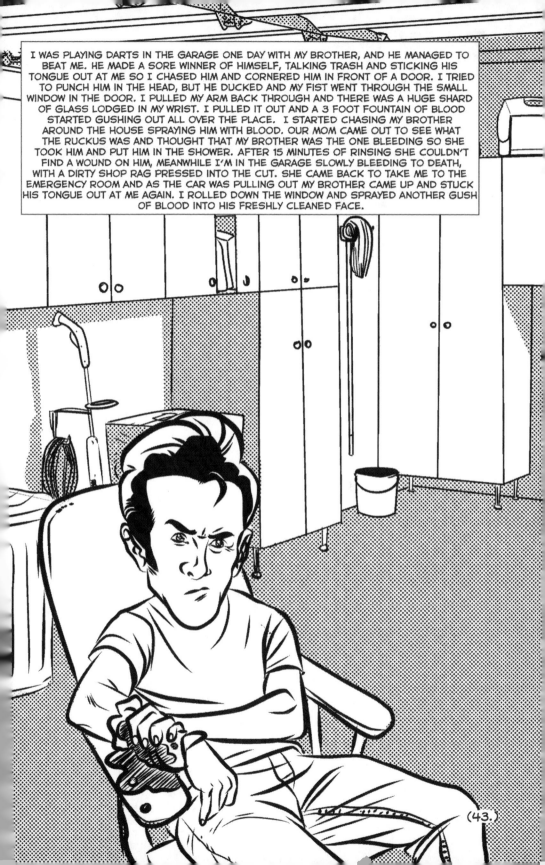

(43.)

LIE 5:
YOU'RE *NOT* SMART ENOUGH.

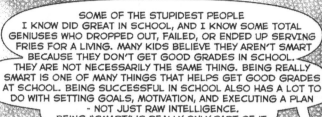

SOME OF THE STUPIDEST PEOPLE I KNOW DID GREAT IN SCHOOL, AND I KNOW SOME TOTAL GENIUSES WHO DROPPED OUT, FAILED, OR ENDED UP SERVING FRIES FOR A LIVING. MANY KIDS BELIEVE THEY AREN'T SMART BECAUSE THEY DON'T GET GOOD GRADES IN SCHOOL. THEY ARE NOT NECESSARILY THE SAME THING. BEING REALLY SMART IS ONE OF MANY THINGS THAT HELPS GET GOOD GRADES AT SCHOOL. BEING SUCCESSFUL IN SCHOOL ALSO HAS A LOT TO DO WITH SETTING GOALS, MOTIVATION, AND EXECUTING A PLAN - NOT JUST RAW INTELLIGENCE. BEING "SMART" IS REALLY ONLY PART OF IT.

I THOUGHT YOU WERE EITHER SMART OR YOU'RE NOT?

ALMOST EVERYBODY KNOWS THE KID WHO GETS B'S AND C'S AND THEN GETS A 1300 ON HIS SAT.

HE'S OBVIOUSLY SMART, BUT DOESN'T DO JACK IN THE CLASSROOM. HE IS PROOF THAT BEING SMART ISN'T ALL IT TAKES FOR ACADEMIC DOMINATION. YOU MAY NOT BE VERY SUCCESSFUL IN SCHOOL RIGHT NOW, BUT THAT'S BECAUSE YOU'RE NOT DOING THE RIGHT THINGS.

WHAT THINGS?

IT'S JUST A MATTER OF LEARNING THE RIGHT STRATEGIES AND EMPLOYING THEM. (SEE BOOK TWO)

YOU CAN GET GRADES AS GOOD AS YOU WANT, IF YOU'RE WILLING TO WORK HARD. I TEACH SAT PREP AND SOME OF MY STUDENTS HAVE ACHIEVED 300 POINT SCORE IMPROVEMENTS BY UTILIZING THE RIGHT STRATEGIES. THEY DIDN'T BECOME ANY "SMARTER" BY TAKING A TWELVE-HOUR COURSE: THEY JUST LEARNED HOW TO MAKE THE MOST OF THE BRAINS THEY ALREADY HAD.

PRETTY SNEAKY, JANTZ

(45.)

THIS IS THE WAY I SEE IT. IF YOU BELIEVE THE LIE THAT YOU CAN'T PERFORM WELL IN SCHOOL BECAUSE YOU'RE "NOT SMART ENOUGH," YOU'RE DIZZY FROM RIDING THE NOT-SO-MERRY-GO-ROUND I LIKE TO CALL THE *WHEEL OF MISFORTUNE.* NO MATTER WHAT INTELLECT YOU POSSESS, YOU DON'T WANT TO BE ON THE WHEEL OF MISFORTUNE. THAT'S A KID WHO DOESN'T SET GOALS, ISN'T MOTIVATED, PERFORMS POORLY, AND GETS A BAD ATTITUDE, ONLY TO AVOID SETTING ANY GOALS AND REPEATS THE SAME CYCLE.

THE ACADEMIC WHEEL OF MISFORTUNE

I DON'T GIVE A CRAP

I DON'T DO CRAP

I DO CRAPPY WORK

I FEEL LIKE CRAP

I'LL DO THAT CRAP LATER

I DON'T PLAN FOR CRAP

UNLESS YOU LIKE FAILURE, SUCCESS IS A PRETTY DESIRABLE THING. MOST SUCCESS BREEDS MORE SUCCESS. EVERY EVENT IN YOUR LIFE IS REGISTERED SOMEWHERE INSIDE YOU. EVERY SUCCESS AND EVERY FAILURE IS RECORDED.

NOT JUST THE GOOD ONES?

NOPE. I HEARD A STORY ABOUT A GIRL ONCE WHO WAS ON A FIRST DATE AT A PIZZA PLACE.

WHILE PRETENDING TO LOOK INTERESTED IN WHATEVER HER DATE WAS SAYING, SHE GRABBED WHAT SHE THOUGHT WAS THE SUGAR TO SWEETEN HER TEA. AFTER A COUPLE SHAKES... SHE TOOK A SIP.

IT TOOK EVERYTHING SHE HAD NOT TO PULL AN OLD FAITHFUL AND SPIT EVERYTHING RIGHT BACK ON THE THE TABLE. SHE'D SPRINKLED RED PEPPER FLAKES IN HER DRINK AND RUINED THE WHOLE THING. SHE ENDED UP DRINKING THE WHOLE THING BECAUSE SHE DIDN'T WANT TO LET ON ABOUT HER MISTAKE.

OK, STAY WITH ME HERE. YOUR ACADEMIC LIFE IS LIKE ONE BIG GLASS OF TEA. WHEN YOU SUCCEED AT SOMETHING, IT GETS A LITTLE SWEETER. THE MORE YOU SUCCEED, THE BETTER IT TASTES...

NOT TOO SWEET, I HOPE.

...BUT THROW IN ONE FAILURE -- ONE FAILED TEST, ONE MISSED HOMEWORK ASSIGNMENT -- AND IT'S LIKE YOU'VE MIXED IN A RED PEPPER FLAKE. IF YOU FAIL A LOT, THE WHOLE THING STARTS TO TASTE LIKE CRAP PRETTY DARN QUICK. IT TAKES MORE SUGAR (IE, ACADEMIC SUCCESS) TO COVER UP THAT BAD TASTE.

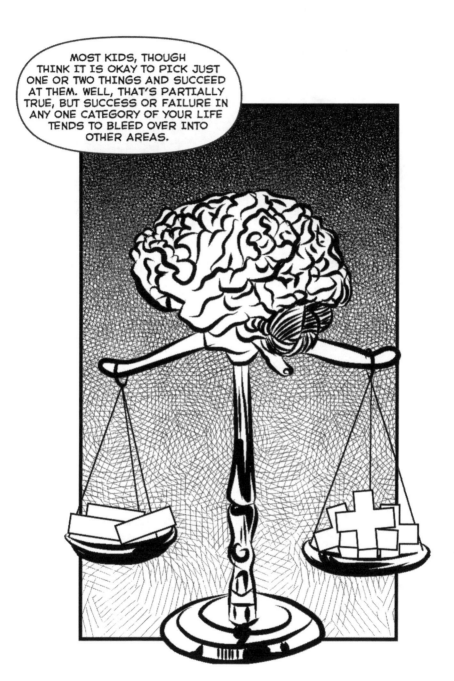

(49.)

LIE

LIE 6:
YOU'RE GONNA BE A SUPERSTAR.

I PLAYED HOCKEY IN COLLEGE AND WAS 6 FT, 195 LBS. AND I COULD *CRUSH* YOUR SKULL IN MY BARE HANDS.

SOUNDS LIKE SOME ANGER ISSUES, JANTZ!

NO, NOT AT ALL. HERE'S MY POINT: WHERE DID THAT GET ME? DID I GET TO PLAY IN THE NHL? NOPE.

NEITHER DOES ANYONE ELSE.

NO ONE?

WELL ALMOST NO ONE, AND ONLY 5% OR SO OF THE ONES WHO DO MAKE IT BECOME HOUSEHOLD NAMES. DO YOU KNOW WHAT AN ANOMALY IS?

"A" IS A PREFIX THAT MEANS WITHOUT OR NOT. "NOMALY" COMES FROM "NOM" -TO NAME (I.E. NOMINATION) ANOMALY MEANS NOT NAMED, - YOU CAN'T EVEN NAME ONE.

PEOPLE WHO PLAY PROFESSIONAL SPORTS ARE MUTANTS. GENETIC FREAKS. ANOMALIES. IF YOU ARE ONE OF THESE PEOPLE YOU'D KNOW BY AGE 15. IF YOU DON'T KNOW BY NOW, YOU AREN'T ONE OF THEM.

HOW DO I KNOW? BECAUSE I HAD AN AVERAGE AMOUNT OF TALENT AND OUTWORKED EVERYONE AROUND ME, AND I NEVER GOT *CLOSE* TO THE PROS.

(53.)

TIME FOR...

ANOTHER
TRUE STORY OF
JANTZI

WHEN I WAS A KID, FIREWORKS WERE MUCH MORE POWERFUL THAN THEY ARE TODAY. THE OLD M-80S WERE ORIGINALLY MADE TO SIMULATE EXPLOSIVES IN MILITARY EXERCISES AND THE LEGEND GOES THAT THEY WERE EQUIVALENT TO A QUARTER STICK OF DYNAMITE. WHO KNOWS -THEY EVEN LOOKED LIKE LITTLE TUBES OF TNT. WE WERE SUCH RESPONSIBLE LITTLE BOYS...WHAT TROUBLE COULD WE POSSIBLY GET INTO WITH MILITARY-GRADE EXPLOSIVES? AFTER BLOWING UP ALL THE SMALL ANIMALS WE COULD FIND, WE DECIDED TO THROW THE M-80S AT PASSING CARS. WE HID IN A DITCH, LIT THE FIRECRACKERS AND TOSSED THEM BLINDLY INTO THE STREET WHEN WE HEARD A CAR COMING. I CHUCKED ONE, BUT INSTEAD OF JUST SCARING THE DRIVER, IT ACTUALLY WENT INTO THE OPEN PASSENGER WINDOW. WHEN IT EXPLODED, A PIECE OF THE GUY'S SEAT WAS EXPELLED FROM THE CAR! BOY WAS THE DRIVER MAD! HE HIT THE BRAKES, SLAMMED THE CAR INTO PARK RIGHT IN THE MIDDLE OF THE STREET, FLUNG OPEN THE DOOR AND STARTED CHASING US LIKE SOME SORT OF RABID SASQUATCH. HE HOUNDED US FOR ALMOST AN HOUR THROUGH THE WOODS. EVENTUALLY WE LOST HIM AND DOUBLED BACK TO HIS CAR, THAT WAS STILL RUNNING WITH THE DOOR WIDE OPEN IN THE MIDDLE OF THE STREET!

LIE 7:
PEER PRESSURE IS BAD.

ONE THING I AM VERY PROUD OF WAS HOW I TREATED OTHER PEOPLE. FOR EXAMPLE, I NEVER LET ANYONE EAT ALONE IN THE CAFETERIA. WHY? BECAUSE THAT WOULD SUCK TO BE THEM. PRETTY SOON PEOPLE LIKE THAT MIGHT COME TO SCHOOL IN A TRENCHCOAT AND YOU KNOW WHAT HAPPENS NEXT.

I WOULD WALK OVER AND INVITE THESE PEOPLE TO SIT WITH ME AT LUNCH. IF THEY REFUSED, I'D EITHER ABDUCT THEM OR I'D JUST MOVE MY GROUP TO THEIR TABLE.

WHAT IF THEY JUST WANTED TO BE ALONE?

NOBODY WANTS TO BE ALONE! GET A GRIP.

NOW WHAT ELSE COMES UP FOR YOU?

I THINK IT'S PRETTY COOL TO REACH OUT LIKE THAT.

THAT'S JUST HOW I WANTED TO BE TREATED. REJECTION SUCKS.

ISN'T THAT WHAT PEER PRESSURE IS ALL ABOUT, REJECTION AND ACCEPTANCE? SEE, YOU CAN BE A TOOL, OR AN INSTRUMENT OF COOLNESS.

BACK TO OUR TOPIC. YOU KNOW WHAT WOULD HAPPEN IF SOMEONE IN OUR LITTLE GROUP WAS UNCOMFORTABLE WITH SITTING WITH THE UNPOPULAR KID? YUP. HE GOT THE LOOK.

WHAT LOOK?

THE "CONFORM, OR YOU'RE SITTING ALONE" LOOK. I'D USE PEER PRESSURE TO GET PEOPLE TO DO WHAT WAS RIGHT. NOW WHAT YOU'VE GOT TO DO IS DECIDE IS IF YOU'RE STRONG ENOUGH TO DO THAT. IF NOT, MAKE SURE YOU PICK YOUR FRIENDS WISELY BECAUSE YOU'RE A FOLLOWER. I'M NOT THAT GUY, BUT YOU MIGHT BE.

(61.)

BUT JANTZI, YOU REJECTED PEOPLE TOO!

YEAH. I DISCRIMINATE ALL THE TIME. HERE'S THE DIFFERENCE. THE KID WHO DIDN'T WANT TO SIT WITH THE OTHER KID DEFINITELY DID SOMETHING WRONG.

THE LONER IS INNOCENT UNTIL PROVEN GUILTY. WE DON'T KNOW HE DID ANYTHING TO DESERVE WHAT HE'S GETTING. ALSO THE KID WHO GOT THE LOOK WAS ALREADY POPULAR AND COULD TAKE IT.

JANTZI, YOU ACT LIKE JUDGE AND JURY.

I'M COMFORTABLE WITH THAT.

MAYBE. OR, IS IT JUST THAT I KNOW WHAT I BELIEVE.

IT'S KIND OF ARROGANT.

I DECIDED A LONG TIME AGO THAT I WAS GOING TO TREAT PEOPLE THE WAY I WANTED TO BE TREATED.

THAT WOULD REQUIRE A LOT OF GENUFLECTION ON YOUR PART.

NICE ONE.

YOU'RE KIND OF PREACHING JANTZI.

OH YEAH, THE DO UNTO OTHERS STUFF I BORROWED FROM SOMEONE ELSE. I NEVER SAID I WAS COMPLETELY ORIGINAL, JUST A GENIUS. THINK ABOUT IT, HOW COULD THIS PHILOSOPHY BE WRONG EVEN IF YOU'RE A COMPLETE HEATHEN.

I'LL TELL YOU THE TRUTH, I DIDN'T ALWAYS KNOW WHERE I WAS GOING IN LIFE. JUST WHO I WOULD GO THERE WITH AND HOW I'D DO IT.

THINK ABOUT WHO YOU HANG OUT WITH. WHERE ARE THEY GOING TO BE IN 10 YEARS? IF YOU ANSWERED CONVENIENCE STORE OR FAST FOOD WORKERS, START PRACTICING NOW FOR WHAT YOU'RE GOING TO BE SAYING A LOT IN THE FUTURE.

WHAT'S THAT?

"DO YOU WANT FRIES WITH THAT?"

I'M NOT SAYING THAT THE PEOPLE WHO HAVE TO SAY THAT ARE BAD PEOPLE, BUT DO YOU REALLY WANT TO BE MAKING MINIMUM WAGE ALL OF YOUR LIFE?

BUT THAT'S ALL SOME PEOPLE CAN DO.

YOU'RE RIGHT, BUT WE'RE TALKING ABOUT YOU, REMEMBER? WHAT IS THE *BEST* THAT YOU CAN DO? IF THAT'S THEIR BEST, THEN SO BE IT.

THE NUMBER ONE REASON NOT TO WORRY ABOUT WHAT PEOPLE SAY ABOUT YOU IS VERY SIMPLE: IN FIVE YEARS YOU WON'T SEE THEM AGAIN. YOU THINK I'M KIDDING, BUT I'M NOT.

(63.)

ABOUT THE AUTHOR

TIM JANTZI, BORN IN BUFFALO, NY, GRADUATED CUM LAUDE FROM THE STATE UNIVERSITY OF NEW YORK AT CORTLAND IN 1983 WITH A BACHELOR OF SCIENCE IN EDUCATION. HE BEGAN HIS TEACHING CAREER IN CHARLESTON, SC. IN 1987 TIM BEGAN TUTORING STUDENTS PART TIME AND SHORTLY THEREAFTER LAUNCHED CAROLINA LEARNING SYSTEMS WHICH LATER BECAME JANTZI TEST PREP AS THE COURSES EXPANDED TO A NATIONAL AUDIENCE. THE VISION WAS TO HELP STUDENTS INCREASE THEIR SAT SCORES BY USING JANTZI'S OWN CURRICULUM CALLED *"STRATEGIES FOR SUCCESS"*. THIS VENTURE HAS GROWN INTO THE LARGEST COURSE OF ITS KIND IN SOUTH CAROLINA. "STRATEGIES FOR SUCCESS" IS NOW TAUGHT IN BOSTON, BUFFALO, INDIANAPOLIS, JACKSONVILLE, AND CHARLESTON. IN 1996, TIM WAS ALSO ASKED TO DESIGN AND TEACH THE SAT PROGRAM FOR THE UNIVERSITY OF SOUTH CAROLINA'S SUMMER CAROLINA CAMP-IN. HE PRESENTED TO THE NATIONAL CONFERENCE ON TESTING IN 1997. TIM JANTZI HAS A VERY UNIQUE STYLE OF TEACHING. HIS DIRECT, NO-NONSENSE APPROACH, COMBINED WITH HIS HUMOR, MAKES HIM AN INSTANT FAVORITE. WITH OVER 25 YEARS OF EXPERIENCE INSTRUCTING THE SAT, IT IS NOT UNCOMMON FOR HIM TO GUESS A STUDENT'S SAT SCORE WITHIN 20 POINTS IMMEDIATELY UPON MEETING THEM. TIM IS MARRIED AND THE FATHER OF THREE CHILDREN.

ALEX SMITH ISN'T AN EXPERT ON THE SAT, BUT HE DOES REALLY LIKE TO DRAW. HE WAS BORN AND MOSTLY RAISED IN CHARLESTON, SC, WITH A FEW LAY-OVERS IN CALIFORNIA, ILLINOIS AND NEW MEXICO HE HAS BEEN A PIZZA COOK, A POST HOLE-DIGGER, A SIGN FABRICATOR, AN ACTOR, AND WORST OF ALL, A SUBSTITUTE TEACHER. THROUGHOUT ALL OF HIS DETOURS, ALEX HAS MANAGED TO KEEP WORKING INTERMITTENTLY AS AN ILLUSTRATOR AND GRAPHIC DESIGNER. HE GOT HIS FIRST PAYING ART JOB IN 1998, AT THE TENDER AGE OF 17, WHEN TIM JANTZI HIRED HIM TO DESIGN FUNNY CHARACTERS FOR HIS SAT PREP COURSE. HE ALSO CO-HOSTS TWO COMIC BOOK PODCASTS: EARTH'S MIGHTIEST PODCAST AND THE BIG ONE COMICS PODCAST. ALEX LIVES WITH HIS WIFE, TWO YOUNG CHILDREN, A DOG, AND TWO UNGRATEFUL CATS OUTSIDE OF CHARLESTON, SOUTH CAROLINA.

Words: Tim Jantzi, M.Ed.
Art: Alex Smith

Editors: Chris Ullery, Amy Maheu

Special Thanks: Carley Anderson, Chase Priest, Dylan Gonzalez

21590247R00039